THOMAS EDISON

A Life From Beginning to End

Copyright © 2017 by Hourly History

All rights reserved.

Table of Contents

Introduction
Edison's Early Life
Personal Life
Menlo Park
The Electric Light
The War of the Currents
Let's Go to the Movies
Other Inventions and Projects
Edison's Later Public Life
Final Years and Death
Edison's Legacy
Conclusion

Introduction

We all know about the lightbulb-over-the-head cartoon. Everyone has seen it. It denotes an idea. If you're old enough, you probably think immediately about the inventor of the lightbulb, Thomas Edison.

There's one small problem with that thought, however; Edison did not truly invent the lightbulb. Many inventors before him had invented incandescent bulbs, but they went no further than to demonstrate how light can produce electricity.

Edison improved on the lightbulb, so much so that his patent made it possible to market it everywhere. That was the genius of Thomas Alva Edison. He has become America's most famous inventor. That is due to the fact that Edison didn't merely invent things, he stepped into the world of business and marketed them as well.

Edison developed many devices that would influence life all around the world. Where would we be today without motion pictures or music caught on CD or DVD? It was Edison who came up with the idea of the phonograph, which inevitably led to our modern digital devices.

Most ingenious of all, Edison applied the principles of mass production and incorporated teamwork on a large scale when it came to working on his inventions. This had never been done before. Edison and his team were granted over 1,000 patents, and most significant of all was what those patents meant to American life and to life all around the world.

Suddenly, Americans had lots of leisure time, and many were looking for new ways to fill up those empty hours. What could be better than to visit a movie theater or buy a phonograph and all the newest records? No longer were people forced to bed when it grew dark; now people everywhere were staying up all night long because electric lights and electric-power distribution were available.

Let us have a look at this remarkable inventor and businessman, Thomas Edison. The next time you pass those high transmission towers or walk past an electrical grid station, know that once a long time ago, there was a man who wanted nothing more than to give you the best life you could have. One that has never before been seen or experienced in the dark centuries of long ago.

Chapter One

Edison's Early Life

"Whether you think you can or think you can't, you're right."

—Henry Ford

Thomas Alva Edison was born on February 11, 1847, in Milan, Ohio. Prior to the Civil War, America was a vastly different place from the country that it is today. After the initial years of American independence and the wars that followed, America was now on a path to prosperity.

Milan was a bustling shipping center. Grain from the farm fields in Ohio was brought here to be sent by canal boat to the Eastern industrial states. Al, as Edison was fondly called by his family, was therefore used to seeing boatmen and sailors all the time.

Edison was the seventh and last child of Samuel and Nancy Edison. Edison's grandfather on his father's side had fought in the War of 1812 and Edison's father was an exile from Canada. He came to the U.S. from Port Huron and settled in Milan. He was a wood shingler, making shingles for houses.

Within the large Edison brood, three siblings died very young and Edison's remaining brothers and sisters were much older than him, so he was raised as if he were an only child. His mother Nancy was a former schoolteacher and taught him at home. Edison learned from his father's extensive library which included the same political hotbed of ideas his father had practiced in Canada as well as books on chemistry and other sciences.

Early in his childhood, Edison developed hearing problems. He suffered from scarlet fever and had recurring ear infections. But, Edison would in the coming years recount various stories as to how his deafness came to be. He recounted how he was thrown off a train with his chemical laboratory when a boxcar caught fire. In later years, he changed the story when he said the conductor had pulled him onto the train by his ears. Most likely, recurrent ear infections from swimming in the dirty waters around Milan was the reason his hearing started to fail.

By 1854 business was failing in Milan, so Edison's family moved to Port Huron in Michigan. The canals had passed their shining moment in American history and were fast being replaced by the railroads.

In Port Huron, Edison was enrolled in school, but this only lasted about three months. His mother caught wind that one of the teachers considered Edison to be "slow"; she promptly withdrew him and started teaching him herself.

Edison learned many things from his father's library. His father would pay him for each book he finished reading, but this did not help Edison to become a fan of mathematics. That fact didn't worry him, though; saying that "I can always hire mathematicians, but they can't hire me."

By the time he was eleven, Edison was cultivating vegetables in his family's large garden plot to supplement their income. He was not all that interested in electricity at this time, preferring chemistry and all of the experiments that went with it. He would conduct his own experiments in the basement of their home, and his mother would often complain about the terrible smells emanating from there.

In time, Edison read his way through his father's extensive library. Then he applied to be a newsboy, selling newspapers on the trains which ran from Port Huron to Detroit.

It didn't take Edison long to discover his talents as a businessman. By the time he was fifteen, Edison was publishing his own newspaper, called the Weekly Herald, which he sold along with the other newspapers. He even went so far as to set up chemical experiments in the baggage car of the train. Unfortunately, there was a fire in that car, and following that incident, he was no longer allowed to go in there.

Being around train stations all the time, Edison became enthralled with telegraphy while watching the telegraph operators at each station. During these early years, Edison realized how business could take him places.

In 1862 after the Battle of Shiloh, headlines were published in the Detroit newspaper telling of the news of casualties and developments in the war. Edison knew hordes of people would want this kind of information; he decided to negotiate with the editors of Detroit Free Press to buy up one thousand copies so that he could distribute them at each train station he worked. He made a large profit.

Edison was taught how to use the telegraph after saving the son of one of the station agents in Michigan. The father was so grateful that Edison had pulled his three-year-old son out of harm's way from a runaway train, that he taught the young entrepreneur how to use the telegraph as a sign of his gratitude.

After the Civil War had ended, Edison moved to Kentucky where he became an employee of Western Union. He still conducted his experiments while working the night shift for the Associated Press. When one of his experiments ended badly and leaked sulfuric acid onto the floor and his bosses' desk one floor below, he was fired.

Working as a telegrapher taught Edison that everything could be improved upon. Out of his knowledge of telegraphy came one of his earliest inventions, that of the stock ticker. Edison's very first patent was for a vote recorder which was granted on June 1, 1869.

It was the start of something big.

Chapter Two

Personal Life

"All creative people want to do the unexpected."

—Hedy Lamarr

Thomas Edison would go on throughout his life to establish and run several companies. It was one of those companies, the News Reporting Telegraph Company, which would set his personal life going in an entirely new direction. With this company, Edison was prepared to transmit business news directly to businessmen; something not done before.

Edison's idea was that businessmen should have access to vital news before it broke in that day's headlines. So it went, that one of the employees he hired was a young 16-year-old girl by the name of Mary Stillwell. On Christmas Day 1871, Thomas and Mary were married. They moved into their own home in Newark, NJ.

During the course of their marriage, the Edisons had three children. Marion Estelle Edison was born in 1873 and a son Thomas Alva Edison Jr. was born in 1876. Edison nicknamed these two children "Dot" and "Dash," a reference to Morse code and his love of this form of communication.

In 1878, a second son was born, William Leslie, who would later graduate from Yale University and follow in his father's footstep to become an inventor. Edison was busy setting up his laboratory at Menlo Park and spent little time at home with his family.

Sadly, in 1884, his wife Mary died at the mere age of 29. There has been speculation as to what killed her; some say a brain tumor, others say that it was a morphine overdose. In those years it was quite common for doctors to prescribe morphine to women for various reasons. Judging by some of her symptoms, it would appear as if she had succumbed to a morphine overdose

Two years later in 1886, when Edison was 39 years old, he married 20-year-old Mina Miller from Akron, Ohio. Her father was also an inventor.

Together, they had three children; Madeleine, born in 1888, Charles born in 1890 and Theodore, born in 1898. Charles would become governor of New Jersey in the 1940s and would take over his father's company and laboratories upon his father's death. Theodore would go on to graduate from the Massachusetts Institute of Technology, and over his lifetime he was credited with 80 patents of his own.

Edison's first three children could often be found at his laboratory in Menlo Park when they were young. Because of Edison's very erratic hours, they would come to the laboratory to play, rather than at home. He was always the absentee father.

In later years, Edison spoke harshly of his two oldest sons. He felt they never amounted to much and whenever they would ask him for money, Edison would recall how they had done him no honor by remaining "absolute illiterates scientifically and otherwise."

Once his first wife died, Edison no longer did his work at Menlo Park. He moved his new family including his young wife Mina into their new home which was close to his new laboratory in West Orange, New Jersey.

Chapter Three

Menlo Park

"There is no expedient to which a man will not resort to avoid the real labor of thinking."

—Sir Joshua Reynolds

Edison created the first industrial research lab in a place which is still called Menlo Park, in Raritan Township, New Jersey. Long before the Menlo Park mall came to be, Edison was there establishing his headquarters for the work which he knew lay in front of him. In fact, the township just next door to Raritan is called Edison, in honor of Thomas Edison's contributions.

By this time Edison had invented the quadruplex telegraph. He was going to sell the rights to it for about $5,000 but wasn't sure of the asking price, so he put it out for bid instead. The Western Union scooped it up for a smooth $10,000 much to Edison's surprise.

Once he had this money in hand, it allowed him to establish his Menlo Park lab. This was the first lab of its kind to be set up specifically for technological innovation and improving his inventions. Edison is credited with most of the inventions created there; even though he had many employees to whom the credit could have gone, as they were responsible for much of the research.

Often Edison would gather his research assistants around him for what we would consider 'brainstorming' sessions. These were intense discussions which he attended for the most part.

Edison chose to work on what he wanted when he wanted, and he chose how to conduct his research. Employees worked six days a week Monday through Saturday, eight hours a day. Of course, if the boss stayed late, they stayed late. There were times when he would work through the night and all the next day, expecting his employees to follow suit.

Because his staff had grown so large, Edison had the means to work on more than one invention at a time. Depending on how interested he was in each invention, Edison would be right there with his assistants taking part in endless experiments. Edison was adept at hiring only the best assistants for his creative endeavors.

One such assistant was William Joseph Hammer, who started working for Edison in 1879. Hammer assisted in experiments during the development of the telephone, iron ore separator, phonograph, electric lighting and electric railway. Hammer worked primarily on the incandescent electric lamp and was Edison's main man for all of the tests and data for the lightbulb.

Another of Edison's key associates was Charles W. Batchelor, a mechanic who would become one of Edison's closest friends and associates. It would be Batchelor who would introduce Nikola Tesla to Edison in the coming years.

As his laboratory in Menlo Park expanded, Edison gave his assistants shares in the various companies created by his inventions. In time his employees would earn far more from their shares than they ever did working for salary under Edison. He was notoriously known for underpaying his assistants. As his companies were created, such as the Edison Lamp Company, the Edison Machine Works, and the Edison Electric Light Company, his assistants would benefit from all of their successes.

In just ten years, Edison's Menlo Park laboratories expanded to occupy two city blocks. Edison wanted a stockroom filled with every type of material ever conceived. It was noted in an 1887 newspaper article that the lab contained "eight thousand kinds of chemicals, every kind of screw made, every size of needle, . . . hair of humans, horses, hogs, . . . silk in every texture, cocoons, various kinds of hoofs, shark's teeth, . . . varnish and oil, ostrich feathers, a peacock's tail, jet, amber, rubber," and the list went beyond that.

Over 1,000 patents hold the name of Thomas Alva Edison. By 1876, Edison was working on improving the microphone, also known as a transmitter in those days, for the telephone. He developed a carbon microphone that used a small amount of carbon that would change resistance with the pressure of sound waves upon it. Edison used this invention to create a telephone which had a much-improved microphone.

This was done for the Western Union. Nine years later, Edison would improve on the Bell Telephone microphone, improving on the loose-contact ground carbon then used. Edison's invention was implemented in 1890 and was used in all telephones until the 1980s.

The invention which would dub him "The Wizard of Menlo Park" in New Jersey would be the phonograph. Because Edison loved working on more than one project at a time, he was able to take ideas from one experiment and apply them someplace else. Because he liked moving his assistants around, Edison was able to come up with his first major invention; the phonograph.

Previously he had been working on the carbon transmitter which would improve the telephone microphone. It was at this time that Edison realized that vibrations picked up by a carbon transmitter could be just as easily applied to a needle instead. This needle could use some sort of physical material to etch the vibrations on to.

Before long, Edison's "talking machine" was created. The phonograph was created in the summer of 1877. Surprisingly, Edison didn't see the potential for mass production at this time. His first phonograph recorded on tinfoil around a grooved cylinder. When Edison presented his idea to the offices of Scientific American, they were so impressed that they held up their latest edition to include this amazing invention.

From that point on, Edison was famous. People believed there was magic coming from those labs in Menlo Park, all due to the Wizard who worked there. Edison believed his phonograph would be best for business purposes and he didn't push it into an entertainment venue. Although his invention brought him vast amounts of newspaper print, at the time Edison received little in the way of money for his efforts.

In 1878 Edison received a patent for his phonograph but didn't do much more to develop it further. It wasn't until other inventors like Alexander Graham Bell and others produced a cylinder-like device that he started to take his invention more seriously.

Edison was on his way to becoming the genius that would live in history as a household name. But, it isn't for the phonograph that Edison is best known. There was another invention that would catapult him to the heights of fame unlike anything known before.

Chapter Four

The Electric Light

"I have not failed. I've just found 10,000 ways that won't work."

—Thomas Edison

To say that Thomas Edison "invented" the light bulb would be a wrong conclusion. In 1878 he started working on a system which was called "electrical illumination" and which he was hoping could compete with what was already out there. Incandescent lamps had already been invented by people such as Humphry Davy, James Bowman Lindsay, Moses G. Farmer, William E. Sawyer, Joseph Swan and Heinrich Gobel. These inventions had all proven useless with their many flaws.

Most early incandescent lights drew far too much power, had very short shelf lives, and were extremely expensive to produce. So, none of them would have been commercially acceptable. Edison knew after studying these past failures that he had to come up with a light bulb which would draw a low amount of current. The voltage would have to be around 110 volts, and the lamp or bulb would require a high resistance.

Edison had formed the Edison Electric Light Company in New York City with the help of financial backing from

J.P. Morgan and members of the Vanderbilt family. Edison's research continued; he knew he had to come up with a workable filament material. At first carbon filaments and then platinum and other metals were used.

By November of 1879, Edison returned to the use of a carbon filament. What Edison and his researchers were able to do was to produce a bulb which burned for 13 1/2 hours. The first successful test of this was done on October 22, 1879. Edison kept at it, improving on his design, he applied for a patent in January of 1880. This patent was for an electric lamp using "a carbon filament or strip coiled and connected to platina contact wires." This was the very first incandescent light ready for commercial use.

On New Year's Eve Edison demonstrated this newly improved incandescent bulb, telling everyone at Menlo Park who witnessed the illumination that "we will make electricity so cheap that only the rich will burn candles." Additional experiments would produce a carbonized bamboo filament that would burn for over one thousand hours.

When Edison had gone on vacation with other members of his scientific team to witness the total eclipse of the sun in Wyoming in 1878, he had been fishing with a bamboo pole. While figuring out which element worked best in his improved light bulb, Edison remembered the strands of the bamboo on the fishing pole. Even while away from the office, Edison was constantly working.

One of the people present at Edison's New Year's Eve lighting party was Henry Villard. Villard's company was building a ship called the Columbia, and he asked Edison to light his new ship. By May 1880 the Columbia was sent to New York City where Edison and his team installed the new lighting system on the ship.

In 1881 an inventor by the name of Lewis Latimer had received a patent for producing carbon filaments in light bulbs. He joined Edison's company in 1884. He also became an expert witness in patent litigation on electric lights.

Suddenly it seemed as if the whole world was waiting for the light bulb. By the time Edison was 35 years old, his light bulb creation was lighting the homes and office buildings on Pearl Street in New York City. Now as his fame grew, Edison found he had less and less time to devote to his experiments. He found himself spending time on battling increasing litigation against him, his company and his patents.

In 1883 the US Patent Office ruled that Edison's patent was invalid. They stipulated that it had been based on the work of one William E. Sawyer. Edison brought a lawsuit claiming no such thing, but the litigation wasn't immediately resolved. In fact, it took six long years.

In October of 1889, a judge ruled that Edison's electric light claim which is based on a filament of carbon of high resistance was valid. In the meantime, Joseph Swan had patented his light bulb in Britain. So, to avoid any conflicts Edison and Swan entered into an agreement, forming a joint company called Ediswan so that the manufacture and marketing of the light bulb could take place in Britain.

Electric lighting was finding itself all around the world. In 1882, the Mahen Theatre in Brno, Czech Republic, was the first public building in the world to use Edison's electric lamps. Edison kept taking old technology, improving on it and marketing it to the world. Because he knew so much about telegraphy, Edison was able to take that knowledge and apply to different mediums; hence, the electric light and the phonograph were both invented from his ideas about telegraphy.

It wasn't enough for Edison to just "invent" the electric light bulb. He then went on to develop an electric utility which he could use to compete with the already existing gas lighting utilities. In 1880, he founded the Edison Illumination Company, and all during that decade, Edison patented a design for electrical power and its safe distribution of his light bulb.

From Edison's generating station on Pearl Street in New York City Edison was now able to provide electrical power to 59 customers in lower Manhattan. Earlier that year, a steam-generated power station was opened in London, England. In 1883, the very first standard electric lighting system utilizing overhead wires began when these wires were strung in Roselle, New Jersey.

Edison was busier than ever, meeting with investors and politicians in the marketing distribution of his inventions. By 1881 he was no longer residing in Menlo Park, although his family would return on vacations there. Menlo Park proved to be a golden place; all during his research years there, Edison came away with over 400 patents in his name. Is it any wonder Menlo Park was referred to as "The Invention Factory?"

Chapter Five

The War of the Currents

"Opportunity is missed by most people because it is dressed in overalls and looks like work."

—Thomas Edison

When Edison established his Edison Illuminating Company in 1882, he did so with the express purpose of competing with the gas utilities already established there. At this time, gas utilities were the leading supplier of electric lighting to homes and businesses. Then, Edison came into direct competition with arc lamp utilities.

Edison's power system ran on direct current or DC power. From the early 1880s arc lighting had become the preferred lighting system in the U.S. Arc lighting ran on alternating current or AC power. These were the majority of electrical systems that were in place at the time. The light emanating from arc lighting systems was uneven and brassy, in fact, many didn't consider arc lighting at all safe for homes.

By the mid-1880s transformers had been developed. It now was possible to transmit AC power over very long distances with the help of thinner and cheaper wires. By doing this, it was possible to decrease the voltage running through the wires. Because of this, people were asking for the new AC power to light up their homes and businesses.

This was what Edison's DC incandescent lamp system had been designed to do. As long as you lived in a big city with a large population, Edison's power supply would suffice. But, for smaller towns and longer distances he was finding himself on the wrong side of the distribution dilemma. Edison's distribution plants couldn't supply power beyond a one-mile radius. There was suddenly a large gap in supplying electrical power to everyone, and AC companies were scrambling to fill that gap.

Here came what became known as the War of the Currents. Edison was a firm believer that AC power was unworkable. AC power depended on high voltages, and Edison said it would never be feasible. By 1886 the Westinghouse Company was fully involved in bringing an AC power distribution system to its customers. Edison began hitting back. He stated that within six months Westinghouse would end up killing a customer after installing their AC system into their home or business. Edison believed there was much work left to be done on the Westinghouse electrical lighting system.

It seems that Edison was dead-set on his DC power system and nothing or no one could persuade him away from it. Some believed Edison wasn't able to understand the abstract theories which made up AC. He was afraid AC systems would end up killing many people, and that it would be the end of electrical lighting systems anywhere.

Add to that the fact that Edison Electric had based their entire design on low-voltage direct current (DC).

They had already installed over 100 systems and to change now was absolutely out of the question. The Westinghouse Company was taking over the electric light business; Edison was fast losing out. In addition to Westinghouse, other companies were on the horizon, such as the Thomson-Houston Electric Company in Massachusetts, which were only adding to Edison's headaches.

In 1884, Edison was visited by a young Croatian man, named Nikola Tesla. This well-dressed gentleman carried a letter of introduction from Charles Batchelor. Tesla had recently emigrated from France and was looking for work in the U.S. He was in luck, and Edison hired Tesla to work at redesigning the company's direct current generators.

Tesla recounted how Edison had offered him a $50,000 bonus if he could successfully improve the generators. Tesla completed the work quickly, but when he asked for his money, Edison told him "you don't understand American humor." But Edison did offer Tesla a $10 per week raise. Tesla promptly quit. But, the conflicts were far from over.

By late 1887 Edison had 121 DC-based power stations to Westinghouse's 68 AC-based power stations. The Thomson-Houston Electric Company had 22 stations. Add to this the fact that other companies were cropping up throughout the country, offering arc lighting and incandescent bulb design, with the equipment to support themselves. Suddenly, there was vast competition which led to patent battles and legal showdowns.

Edison began getting resistance to his DC system, and members of his staff started urging him to make the switch to AC power. Edison firmly believed that both Westinghouse and Thomson-Houston were using AC power to avoid using Edison's patents. He still believed that a DC system was the more cost-efficient way to go.

What Edison did next was to start a campaign to educate the public about AC and DC power. After all, only those with knowledge would be better equipped to make rational decisions. He wanted to show the country how much better his DC system was and how dangerous an AC system could be. Who knew better than the Wizard of Menlo Park?

By the spring of 1888, there had been accidental deaths attributed to the high-voltage current running through high wires. The media picked up on the dangers of AC electricity immediately. This was the perfect time for Edison to start his AC fear-mongering campaign.

Edison teamed up with Harold Brown, an electrical engineer, who was crusading against the perils of AC electric-power systems. Edison even went so far as to aid Brown in the public electrocution of animals to prove his point. He was all for legislation being introduced to limit AC power and to stop its installations.

This "battle of currents" as the media named it, were perpetrated by Edison and Brown against the Westinghouse Company. After all, the public knew little of the dangers of electricity, and if companies were to profit from this new invention, then people should be told the truth. The electric chair was invented at this time as well, to show the dangers of AC electric power.

By the 1890s Edison's attacks against Westinghouse and the Thomson-Houston Company were not very popular with his stockholders. AC power was winning the day as Edison's company was hauling in lesser profits than the AC companies. By 1892 the worst had happened. Thomas Edison had been forced out of control of his company.

With the help of the tycoon J.P. Morgan, Edison General Electric was merged with the Thomson-Houston Company to become General Electric. They now controlled three-quarters of the US electrical business and would be the competition Westinghouse needed to beat them at their game.

Edison's efforts to get the public on his side by making AC electricity out to be dangerous had not worked. Edison couldn't have gone on alone anyway; by 1890 there were over 60 patent-infringement lawsuits against Edison General Electric and Edison himself announced he would be retiring from the lighting business to pursue other ventures.

But by the time General Electric was founded in 1892, the Westinghouse Company was awarded the contract to light up Niagara Falls. This was done with the help of Nikola Tesla, whom Edison had treated so badly.

Regardless of all the lawsuits and company mergers, Edison's star still shined brightly. The public could not think badly of him. He had closed up his research laboratories in Menlo Park and opened a new facility in

West Orange, New Jersey. It would be from here that Edison started working on something besides electric lights. And this invention would bring enchantment to the world.

Chapter Six

Let's Go to the Movies

"I've always said that Thomas Edison invented the movie camera to show people killing and kissing."

—Quentin Tarantino

Back in the late 19th century when Edison was heavily involved in many diverse inventions, life was a lot different from what is experienced today. Because he had turned his head away from the public while involved in litigation and patent infringements, Edison had quickly lost touch with how people were feeling in the culture of 1890s America.

Once his phonograph was invented and marketed there were other inventors making improvements on it without violating any of Edison's patents. This was because citizens were demanding that music be recorded so they could listen to it. Edison still believed a phonograph should never be used for recreational purposes, but only in business for recording and dictation purposes.

There were stage shows in those days, and many enjoyed the burlesque and vaudeville shows that moved around the country. Yet, now that people were able to stay up late in their homes because of electric lighting, they were clamoring for more to do with an evening's entertainment.

By 1888 Edison was working on a device that would "do for the eye what the phonograph does for the ear." He was granted a patent for a motion picture camera or what came to be called the "kinetograph". He left the bulk of the development to his chief photographer William Dickson while Edison worked on the electromechanical design. In fact, the design of the camera actually belongs to Dickson.

The kinetoscope or peep-hole viewer was developed in 1891 by Edison and was initially installed in penny arcades where people could enjoy short films. The kinetoscope was driven by sprockets that pushed a flexible film strip through the device, and suddenly pictures were moving.

In order to see films moving through the kinetoscope, you needed people to produce them. Dickson was the one who constructed a movie studio which he dubbed the "Black Maria." The studio was small, mounted on a turntable and let in plenty of sunlight through its retractable roof, so there was ample light for filming.

Immediately Dickson started creating short films for the general public. Another Edison assistant saw the commercial value in producing such works. It was Tate who purchased a shoe shop on Broadway in New York City and turned the shop into the first kinetoscope parlor. Because the 10 machines that were delivered there didn't have coin slots, he printed up paper tickets for admission. These became the first movie tickets.

Once Tate and his assistants opened the kinetoscope parlor people flocked there to see the latest film. What they didn't want to see was the same film again and again, so Dickson realized that more films were necessary and needed immediately.

During the 1890s, the kinetoscope was finding its way to Europe. First to London, then to Paris and on into Germany, the Netherlands, and Italy.

Meanwhile, Dickson was busy creating short films for the kinetoscope. He was modifying the machine to film longer productions and even recorded prize fights. By this time something other than the kinetoscope was needed. Businessmen came to Edison asking him to develop a motion picture projector. They believed people would love a larger screen and a place to sit and watch their movies.

Edison refused at first to be drawn into a projector project. He thought a projection system would take over his kinetoscope business, and he didn't want to risk it. Besides, right now he needed the money. He was quoted as saying that where the motion picture projector was concerned "there will be a use for maybe 10 of them in the whole United States." Even popular inventors can be wrong.

Without Edison's knowledge or approval, Dickson began working on a projection system of his own along with other entrepreneurs. When Edison got wind of this, Dickson resigned. Who owned what, and whose property rights the projection system belonged to was the source of numerous lawsuits over the ensuing years.

Finally, Edison jumped on board the motion picture train. He even allowed his name to be used for a projection system, the Edison-Vitascope, even though he had next to nothing to do with its development. Edison almost walked away from this latest venture but needed money so badly that he agreed to continue the development of the vitascope.

Once the vitascope debuted, it was a grand success. Again, people were amazed at how one man could just keep on inventing new and amazing inventions that made their lives so comfortable and convenient.

Edison became the head of his own movie studio. Over time the movie studio made almost 1,200 movies. Most of these were short films and gave the public a little of everything; from parades to acrobats to fire engines. There were titles such as Fred Ott's Sneeze (1894), The Kiss (1896), The Great Train Robbery (1903), Alice's Adventures in Wonderland (1910) and the first Frankenstein film in 1910.

When the owners of Luna Park in Coney Island, New York announced they were going to execute Topsy the elephant by electrocution, strangulation, and poisoning, Edison's Studios sent a film crew to catch it all on film. In 1904 the movie Electrocuting an Elephant was released.

Even though Edison himself didn't invent motion pictures, he was still regarded as the man who did. Edison never understood the relevance of this latest invention. He always felt that the projection system should be used for business and training purposes. Edison failed to see the great opportunity in front of him for its tremendous entertainment abilities.

In 1908 Edison started the Motion Pictures Patent Company which brought together nine major motion picture studios. The motion picture industry was in its infancy during these years, and if Edison had seen its potential and all it offered to society in general, all his money problems could have been swept under the rug.

In the end, he lost interest in this new device and didn't turn to it again until there was a need to blend pictures with sound. Even then, he believed talking pictures "spoiled everything" for him. Still, he had a favorite movie (The Birth of a Nation) and his favorite actors were Mary Pickford and Clara Bow.

Chapter Seven

Other Inventions and Projects

"If we worked on the assumption that what is accepted as true really is true, then there would be little hope for advance."

—Orville and Wilbur Wright

During the beginning years of the 20th century when Edison was involved in developing his kinetoscope and motion picture projector, there was another more pressing endeavor that he was devoting most of his time to. In retrospect, this would drain his resources and offer him scant prospect for success. But he was determined anyway.

What Edison was involved in was iron ore mining. He had shown great interest in this field since the 1870s. Once Edison realized he wasn't going to win the Current Wars, he turned his attention elsewhere. In the 1880s, he developed a means of separating iron ore using magnets.

Once Edison had received money for stepping away from his company General Electric, he used the capital to buy an iron ore mine in northern New Jersey in Ogdensburg. This little hamlet tucked away in Sussex

County, NJ was going to be the answer to Edison's money woes. It was there that Edison began to build a system to mine the iron ore.

Edison had developed a number of rollers and crushers that would pulverize rocks as large as 10 tons. He believed this was far more efficient than using dynamite, which was very expensive. Edison even set up himself and his assistants in an old farmhouse in the vicinity rather than having to drive down to West Orange constantly.

However, right from the start, the mining project had problems. Once the giant rollers crushed the rock, it made magnetic extraction very difficult. Not to mention the rock crushers created a lot of thick dust, which didn't blow away in New Jersey's hot, humid summers. Some of his personnel left, so Edison assigned a group of men, seventeen in all, to control the dust problem. Edison was there six days a week, only returning home to his family on Sunday.

In time, huge reserves of iron ore were discovered in the Mesabi Range in northeastern Minnesota. Edison realized at that point that his small iron ore operation was doomed. The ore in Minnesota was easily mined and close to shipping facilities. Combine that with the falling prices of iron ore and Edison's magnetic extractors were no longer feasible.

Even though Edison's steel rollers were no longer used to mine iron ore, they did eventually find a home in Portland Oregon for cement manufacturing. This iron ore venture used up money that Edison could have put into more lucrative projects. He was determined to make his iron ore endeavor successful, so he ignored many ideas where the motion picture projection system and movie studios were concerned.

Another invention that Edison is credited with is the fluoroscope. In the late 1890s, he began experimenting with various materials that would be visible in an x-ray. By 1900 he had invented a fluoroscope that could be manufactured commercially. Edison was using calcium tungstate because this element produced the brightest images on the screen.

But, just a few short years later, Edison left off with his fluoroscopy inventions. Clarence Dally, who was one of Edison's assistants in the lab suffered radiation poisoning from repeated exposure to x-rays; he would eventually die from aggressive cancer. Even Edison damaged one of his eyes with his repeated fluoroscope experiments.

Edison's experiments were crucial to setting the foundations for modern fluoroscopy. The fundamental design of his fluoroscope is still in use today, but Edison became afraid of what x-rays were capable of doing to the human body. He quickly abandoned his endeavors.

Later on, in the 1920s, Edison joined up with Harvey Firestone and Henry Ford to create the Edison Botanic Research Corporation, constructing a lab in Fort Myers, Florida where they conducted rubber experiments. At the time the U.S. was getting its bulk of rubber from countries overseas. Edison wanted to find a way to cultivate rubber in the U.S.

Unlike other experiments, Edison did the majority of the research and planting. He would send soil samples back to his headquarters in West Orange, NJ for further evaluation of the sample rubber residues. His methods were based on a two-part acid-based extraction; latex was derived from the plant material after it was dried and crushed down to powder form. It would take about 17,000 plant samples before Edison could say he found success in the Leavenworth Goldenrod plant.

This plant normally grows 3 – 4 feet tall, and its latex yield is about 5%. By cross-breeding plants, Edison was able to produce products twice the size with a latex yield of 12%. In October 1931, Edison announced he was close to finding a domestic source of rubber. But sadly, before the month was over Edison had died. His brother-in-law John would continue work on the rubber project until it was finally shut down in 1936.

Chapter Eight

Edison's Later Public Life

"When you have exhausted all possibilities, remember this. You haven't."

—Thomas Edison

From the moment Edison marketed his light bulb over all the others that had come before him, his name would become a household name throughout the world. He would always be known as a man of great innovation, a spark of genius, determination, and quality.

As the years went by, hundreds of companies would come to carry his name, even though they had no affiliation with Edison whatsoever. As early as the 1890s, Edison filed a lawsuit against The Edison Chemical Company, which wasn't associated with him at all. Another businessman with the same last name had named his company thus.

Edison was certainly adept at marketing inventions, the light bulb being a prime example of those skills. He didn't so much as "invent" the light bulb, but he knew how to market it better than his competitors. Throughout his long career, he created many businesses; his patents were licensed, his products were manufactured, equipment was built, and whole industries sprang up where once there was nothing.

To think that one man could be interested in telegraphy, electricity, fluoroscopy, rubber, motion pictures and more is a testament to the innovation of Thomas Edison. He maintained controlling interests in other companies and sold them for profit. There were some which merged with each other, others which formed the basis of his company General Electric, and some who continued operating on their own.

Edison, unlike other inventors of his day, did not do all of this alone. His genius lay in hiring only the very best assistants, many of whom stayed with him for decades; these men knew Edison well and were adapted to his work schedules and quirks. Some, like Nikola Tesla would come and go quickly.

Beginning in the 1870s and 1880s Edison created and ran companies that established him as the primary producer and distributor of incandescent lights. It wasn't just the light bulb which was manufactured. There were companies that produced wires, insulators, connectors, sockets and the equipment to produce all of these. Edison was also right there when it came to producing current and how it was distributed to customers.

Additionally, Edison had his network of companies that would conduct his research, develop products, research new markets, build systems, as well as collect the fees that went along with providing electric lights to homes and businesses. Most of these companies would become the General Electric Company, and because

Edison stubbornly refused to stay out of a war of currents, he lost control of his company, as well as all of the patents that went with it.

Chapter Nine

Final Years and Death

"I never did a day's work in my life. It was all fun."

—Thomas Edison

Edison lived near to Henry Ford in their Fort Myers, Florida community. The two men had met years before when Ford worked as an engineer for the Edison Illuminating Company way back in the 1890s. Edison and Ford became good friends in their later years, usually taking yearly motor camping trips from 1914 to 1924.

Edison continued to work when most men would have been long retired. In 1928 Edison brought direct current power to the Lackawanna Railroad when they introduced an overhead catenary system. This was the cable running along the track above the train from which the wire is suspended.

When the first train of this kind left the Hoboken, NJ train station, Edison was at its helm. This particular set of train cars would run in northern New Jersey for the next 54 years until they were retired in 1984.

When Europe entered into the First World War in 1914 Edison urged his fellow citizens to stay prepared. He believed that technology would be the future of war. Edison was named the head of the Naval Consulting

Board in 1915 which was the government's way of bringing science into the defense program. Mostly this board was an advisory one, but there was a research laboratory which was implemented in 1923 for the Navy.

During the war, Edison still busied himself with naval research. In particular, he was interested in submarine detection. He made many suggestions and recounted his inventions to the Navy regarding this, but for the most part, he was ignored.

In the 1920s Edison's health was worsening, and he was spending most of his time at home. Because all of his life had been spent in his laboratories, his relationship with his grown children was a strained one. Charles Edison was president of Thomas A. Edison Inc. Stuck at home, Edison would have loved to travel to his West Orange labs and conduct more experiments, but it was not possible.

His good friend Henry Ford had reconstructed Edison's research factory at Menlo Park as a museum at Greenfield Village, Michigan. It opened during the fiftieth anniversary of Edison's electric light in 1929.

There was a huge celebration called Light's Golden Jubilee at Menlo Park, and it was co-hosted by Ford and General Electric. A dinner was held in Edison's honor, and attendees included President Hoover, John D. Rockefeller Jr., George Eastman, Marie Curie and Orville Wright.

Finally, on October 18, 1931, Edison died from complications of diabetes. He had suffered from this disease for a long time, and by late summer he was also having kidney problems. He seemed to recover from this only to become semi-comatose as death grew near. It was in his home Glenmont in West Orange, NJ which he had purchased for his bride Mina in 1886 as a wedding present, that he drew his last breath.

It was estimated that 40,000 people paid their respects to Edison where he was laid out in his laboratory in West Orange. Henry Ford couldn't get himself to enter the room where his good friend was resting. The First Lady was there on behalf of her husband, as was Harvey Firestone.

President Hoover urged all citizens to extinguish their lights at ten p.m. as a tribute to Edison. The president is quoted as saying "this demonstration of the dependence of the country upon electrical current for its life and health is in itself a monument to Mr. Edison's genius." For one minute on that fateful day, most of the country did go dark. Edison was buried in Rosedale Cemetery in West Orange.

Edison's estate was not as large as some people would think. It was estimated to be around $12 million, which in its day was an immense amount of money. Edison died at the height of the Great Depression, and by the time his will was probated, there was maybe $1.5 million left. As for his surviving companies, they didn't do so well either.

Thomas A. Edison Inc. did eventually merge with the McGraw Electric Company of Chicago. The name changed to McGraw-Edison. Unlike his friends, Edison had a paltry few million compared to their rich endowments of one hundred million or more. Many of their personal savings were in the tens of millions as well.

Most of Edison's savings were always plugged back into his companies during his lifetime.

As a testament to his scientific life, Edison's last breath is supposedly contained in a test tube which resides at the Henry Ford Museum. A plaster cast of his face and hands was also made.

Over time there were many honors, awards, tributes, memorials, and museums dedicated to Edison's legacy. In 2008 Thomas Edison was inducted into New Jersey's Hall of Fame. In 1920 the United States Navy awarded Edison the Navy Distinguished Service Medal. He entered the National Academy of Sciences in 1927. In 1915 he was awarded the Franklin Medal at the Franklin Institute in Philadelphia, PA. In 1983 the U.S. Congress designated February 11, Edison's birthday, as National Inventor's Day.

In 2010, Edison was even awarded a technical Grammy Award. In 2011 he was inducted into the Entrepreneur Walk of Fame and named a great Floridian by the governor and cabinet in Florida.

Then there are the people and places named for Edison. In New Jersey, there is the town of Edison, which sits approximately 20 miles southwest of NYC. Thomas Edison State University was established for adult learners and was one of the earliest long-distance schools. There are numerous high schools named after the famed inventor. The Hotel Edison in New York City was lit up in 1931, and Edison was there to turn on the lights himself.

Three bridges around the country have been named in Edison's honor; the Edison Bridge in New Jersey, the

Edison Bridge in Florida and the Edison Bridge in Ohio. Edison was honored with his own star in space, where his name is commemorated as asteroid 742 Edisona.

Edison's home Glenmont in West Orange has been maintained by the National Park Service and named the Edison National Historic Site. His laboratories and workshops also include a reconstructed "Black Maria" which was the world's first movie studio. There are statues bearing his name, and companies all over the U.S. with Edison in their name, too.

In 1904 a group of Edison's associates and friends created the Edison Medal. Four years later, the American Institute of Electrical Engineers entered into an agreement to have the Edison Medal presented as their highest award. This medal is awarded every year "for a career of meritorious achievement in electrical science, electrical engineering or the electrical arts."

Chapter Ten

Edison's Legacy

"If we did all the things we are capable of, we would literally astound ourselves,"

—Thomas Edison

Thomas Edison was many things in his lifetime. Arguably, one of his best—and worst—qualities was that he was a persistent man. Sometimes his stubbornness would get in his way, as when he lost the "war of currents" which left him financially bankrupt. In other ways, this bullheadedness served him well; for it was this that made Edison return again and again to perfecting his experiments.

Edison brought many insightful inventions into the world. But, often he couldn't see the good they would become, and often he got in his own way when insisting something must be done the way he envisioned it.

One shining example of this is his phonograph. He insisted that it only be used in business and research endeavors. He saw it as a wonderful learning tool, where films for education could be seen by all. Edison couldn't envision the mass public using his glorious invention for entertainment purposes. He would always back away from endorsing its use in this manner.

Edison, because he was the inventor, thought he knew what was best for people. When he continued thinking the way he did about what his inventions were good for, people turned to other competitors for their fun. Still, Edison held onto his beliefs.

When it was shown that AC current would be much more workable over DC current, Edison wouldn't budge. He resolutely refused to see the futility of his thinking when it came to DC current. Direct current power systems would never have been able to power everything for long distances and many other inventions such as the railroads would never have prospered as they did on DC current alone.

When he was wrong, he refused to see it. He wouldn't admit it either; rather he would personally attack those who were bringing these revelations to his attention. Innovators such as George Westinghouse and Nikola Tesla were sorely verbally abused by Edison which started giving him a reputation for being a mean man. He even went so far as to conduct unnecessary tests, electrocuting dogs, for instance, to show the public how dangerous AC high-voltage power could be.

Long after scientific data had proved his theories wrong, Edison would still insist they were right. Perhaps it had everything to do with the fact that so many of his inventions were glorious failures at the onset. There were some, such as the incandescent bulb which he made work, but there were others which he kept improving on, with no possible way for them to ever work. Still, he kept at it.

Thomas Edison has been gone for over eighty-five years now. As inventors go, he is one of the world's most famous and most creative. His innovations have been improved on and duplicated all over the world. This American-born inventor seems to define the word.

In Edison's lifetime alone, he amassed 2,332 patents from his inventions. Over a thousand of those were from the United States. You would think that the legacy of his patents would be enough, but for a man such as Thomas Edison, there was so much more.

In taking a look through all of his inventions, many scientists and historians regard the phonograph as Edison's greatest invention. This was his personal favorite, and he was constantly returning to it over the years to improve its quality. When Edison recorded himself as saying "Mary had a little lamb" he was completely stunned, as were his staff, when they heard the first replay.

Edison's motion picture camera was similar to his phonograph box, but this device came equipped with a spiral arrangement of 1/16th-inch photographs which spun on a cylinder. When George Eastman came up with celluloid film, Edison used it to improve on his motion picture camera. The films were cut into strips with perforated edges; creating the iconic shape that most of us picture when we think about a film roll.

Edison's vote recorder was invented when he was a mere 22 years old. He was still working as a telegrapher at the time but already loved tinkering with new ideas. This new invention would become the new way the US Congress would cast votes; no longer would a simple "yay" or "nay" suffice. This device connected to the clerk's desk where all of the votes were recorded.

There were Edison's mining devices, giant magnets and steel rollers which he devised to crush rocks. He grew rubber plants and at the end of his life became involved with Henry Ford's automobiles, encouraging the development of the internal combustion engine, which all by itself, would transform culture around the globe.

The one "invention" that Edison is known for above all others is the light bulb. This is Edison's greatest legacy. He didn't invent the incandescent light; it was already there when he started working on it. What he did do was design cheaper bulbs that could be easily manufactured, last a long time and were cheap to buy. What Edison did was to introduce a bamboo filament into a vacuum bulb with lower voltage. The rest, as they say, is history.

In history, unbelievably, is where the light bulb will most likely end up. As the 21st century has dawned, the need for newer lighting technologies has been on the horizon for some time. Instead of the old light bulb, fluorescent and LED technology is much more energy efficient and last longer that Edison's incandescent bulb.

As these older technologies are replaced by newer ones, it must be remembered that they would never have been made possible if not for the dogged abilities of such men like Thomas Edison.

Edison's legacy was one of being both an inventor and an innovator. He had the innate ability to go beyond what was there, and by improving on it through countless experiments, Edison made it that much better.

What set Edison apart from so many other inventors and scientists was that he was able to figure out something from its very inception, then move it through the patent stage where research was performed, all the way to the development and marketing of that particular invention. Many of his contemporaries never stayed with a project as he did. Edison would involve himself in all stages of his inventions.

Under Edison, the laboratory would be transformed into something much more than merely hammering out solutions to problems. In fact, up until this point scientists and inventors had shops. It wasn't until Edison came along that the shop would be transformed into a laboratory. From here basic research would be conducted and compiled.

One of Edison's best qualities is that what he couldn't find in books, he conducted his own experiments to find out. It would be through rudimentary research, countless hours of experimentation that Edison would revolutionize how manufacturing and research would be carried out from that point forward.

To go along with his research facilities, Edison started to employ some of the brightest minds around. They would become a part of his legacy, for, without their dedicated service, much of what he envisioned could never have seen the light of day.

Edison conducted business like a businessman. He had teams of experimenters, assistants, and machinists who were absolutely essential to running his operations. It was within these teams that some of his most innovative technologies would be created and go on to transform the world. Throughout it all, Edison remained involved in everything that was going on. He wasn't an absentee landlord or someone who popped in now and then to see how things were going. He was right there working alongside his crews, watching and developing along with them.

Unlike many of his contemporaries such as Henry Ford and Harvey Firestone, Edison did not involve himself in philanthropic activities. He wasn't one to support charities any more than he established a foundation in his name. Possibly, because Edison never really retired, he didn't have the time or the inclination for any of it.

Conclusion

In 1997, Life Magazine published a special double issue called "The 100 Most Important People in the Last 1000 Years." Edison was placed first in this long list of luminaries.

Thomas Edison was one of the greatest inventors of all time, if not the greatest inventor ever. That is because he did one thing and one thing only; he dreamed of visions not yet seen in American culture, and he made those visions come true.

Thomas Edison lit up the world. He was never about making vast amounts of money, however nice that would have been for his many inventions. He was all about innovation; he could look at something and see the potential for it to become so much more. He believed that it was his work and nothing more that made him the famous man he became.

So many people, famous and not so famous would find their way to his laboratory at Menlo Park to gaze upon the man who made all of his inventions work. He was dubbed The Wizard of Menlo Park, and even today, he is still in a class of his own. We live in the modern world; you can thank Thomas Edison for getting us there.

Made in the USA
Las Vegas, NV
17 October 2023

79254065R10030